THE HISTORY NEWS

EXPLORERS

Author: MICHAEL JOHNSTONE ✳ *Consultant:* SHANE WINSER

DEAR READER,

THROUGHOUT THE CENTURIES, *THE HISTORY NEWS* HAS ALWAYS BEEN THE FIRST TO BRING YOU THE BIG STORIES. NO WONDER WE HAVE LONG BEEN THE WORLD'S FAVORITE NEWSPAPER.

RECENTLY, WE DECIDED IT WAS TIME TO CELEBRATE OUR THOUSANDS OF YEARS OF NEWSGATHERING BY LOOKING BACK THROUGH PAST COPIES OF *THE HISTORY NEWS*. NOT SURPRISINGLY, WE FOUND THAT MANY OF THE MOST EXCITING STORIES WERE ABOUT EXPLORERS — THEIR TRIUMPHS AND TRAGEDIES, THEIR DRAMAS AND DISASTERS. THEY TRAVELED AND WE REPORTED.

WE HAD SUCH A FASCINATING TIME READING ABOUT ALL THEIR ADVENTURES THAT WE FELT SURE YOU WOULD ENJOY THEM, TOO. SO HERE IT IS — *THE HISTORY NEWS*'S SPECIAL EDITION ON EXPLORERS AND EXPLORATION!

HAVE AN EXCITING JOURNEY!

THE EDITOR IN CHIEF   *Michael Johnstone*

A NOTE FROM OUR PUBLISHER
Of course, as we all know, newspapers didn't exist as long as 3,500 years ago.
But if they had, we're sure that *The History News* would have been the one
everybody was reading! We hope you enjoy reading it, too.

SCHOLASTIC INC.
New York Toronto London Auckland Sydney

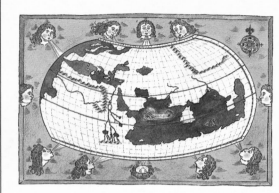

WHAT IS EXPLORATION?

THE DICTIONARY DEFINES EXPLORATION AS "AN ORGANIZED TRIP INTO UNFAMILIAR REGIONS."

BUT THAT CAN'T BE THE WHOLE STORY. WHAT COULD POSSIBLY DRIVE PEOPLE TO RISK THEIR LIVES TO TRAVEL INTO UNCHARTED LANDS, OR TO SAIL INTO UNKNOWN OCEANS?

WHAT SPURRED SOME WAS A NEED TO DISCOVER NEW PLACES TO SETTLE. OTHERS TOOK TO THEIR BOATS HOPING TO FIND NEW PEOPLE TO TRADE WITH. PERHAPS CONQUEST WAS THE SPARK THAT FIRED EXPLORATION, OR MAYBE THE CAUSE WAS A SIMPLE INTEREST IN SEEING FOR ONESELF WHAT LAY BEYOND THE HORIZON.

BUT FOR MANY OF THESE BRAVE MEN AND WOMEN THERE WAS ALSO THE DESIRE TO BE FIRST — TO GO SOMEWHERE NO ONE HAD EVER BEEN BEFORE, OR TO DO SOMETHING NO ONE ELSE HAD EVER DONE.

AND THIS IS WHAT WE LOOKED FOR WHEN CHOOSING THE STORIES FOR THIS EDITION OF *THE HISTORY NEWS*. ALL THE EXPLORERS WE INCLUDED HERE OPENED UP OUR PLANET IN ONE WAY OR ANOTHER.

ACROSS THE SEAS

Illustrated by PETER VISSCHER

ALL ABOARD: Men and women pack as many supplies as possible into their canoe in preparation for a perilous journey into the immense Pacific Ocean.

HERE AT *The History News* we think the greatest explorers of all time were the Polynesians, who set off into the vast Pacific Ocean 3,500 years ago. Our sailing expert picks up the story.

WHEN I WAS asked to write this article, I tried to imagine what it must have been like to sail off into a vast open ocean with no compass or sea charts to guide me and no way of knowing where the next land lay.

Yet the Polynesians did exactly that — and not just once, but many, many times.

At first, these people lived only among the islands of Papua New Guinea. But by 1500 B.C., the lands were becoming crowded. So some of the people moved on, hoping to find that there were lands beyond the horizon, where they could settle.

We now know that there are thousands of islands throughout the Pacific Ocean. But they are scattered far and wide — to find any of these islands without the navigational instruments we rely on today would be like trying to find a needle in a haystack.

NEW HORIZONS

Yet over the generations, the Polynesians spread across this whole area. They learned how to use changes in the winds and the ocean currents, along with the positions of the sun and the stars, to help guide them.

As they sailed, they looked for signs that land was near. They searched for clouds in a clear sky, as these usually form over an island. And they followed the flight of birds that they knew roosted on land at night.

For 2,000 years, canoe followed canoe across the Pacific Ocean in this way. Even for a sailor today, these journeys would be dangerous and bold. I can only salute those brave pioneers — the Polynesians. ✳

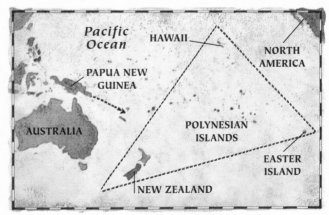

FAR AND AWAY: Over thousands of years, the Polynesians gradually settled on all of the islands within this triangle.

HANNO'S A HERO

Illustrated by CHRIS MOLAN

BACK IN 470 B.C., Hanno, one of the first explorers known to us by name, set sail to discover what lay beyond the lands he knew. A reporter from *The History News* went with him.

AS WE SAILED out from Carthage in North Africa I wondered if I were mad.

True, the leader of our expedition was Captain Hanno, an expert sailor and an important man in the port of Carthage. And I was on a voyage with the Phoenicians — known for hundreds of years as the best sailors on the Mediterranean Sea.

But even for the bold Phoenicians, what Hanno was planning to do was terrifying. He wanted to travel through the Strait of Gibraltar, the narrow stretch of water that lies between southern Spain and North Africa, and out into the Atlantic Ocean.

All Phoenicians believe the end of the world lies just beyond this strait, but that didn't bother Hanno. He was intent on exploring along the coast of West Africa.

ADVENTURES BEGIN

The first part of our trip passed smoothly enough. Hanno led his fleet of 60 ships along the coast, stopping six times to leave behind ships and settlers to build trading colonies for Carthage.

This done, Hanno was free to explore. We sailed south along the coast, and at the mouth of a great river, turned inland. We explored until the river was so shallow and the water teemed with so many crocodiles that we had to turn back.

At times we stopped to search for supplies. On one island we were attacked by large fierce creatures which looked almost human — beasts we called gorillas.

But my most vivid memory was when we sailed near an exploding mountain. This blew up with such force that red-hot rocks flew into the air and a river of liquid fire cascaded into the sea.

When at last we turned for home, I knew we were lucky to be alive. I also knew that I was fortunate to have been a part of this daring expedition.

Thanks to Hanno's courage, we had been to places unknown to any of the peoples of the Mediterranean Sea. We would be welcomed as heroes on our return. ✶

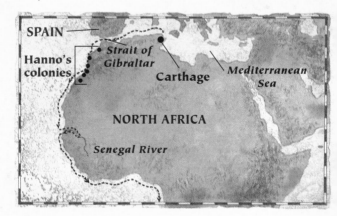

FIERY FOUNTAIN: An erupting volcano was just one of the many dangers Hanno faced.

From *The History News*, 470 B.C.

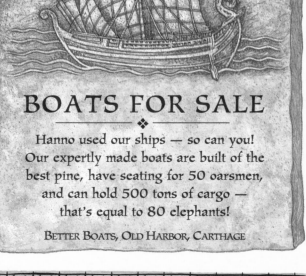

AROUND THE BEND: Hanno's route along West Africa.

THE WORLD BEYOND

Illustrated by RICHARD BERRIDGE

BEFORE 138 B.C., the great empire of China knew nothing of the wealthy lands in the West. Then a man named Chang Chi'en went on a journey that forged a link that lasted a thousand years. He talked to *The History News* on his return.

ACCORDING TO an old Chinese proverb, even the longest journey starts with one step. Back in 138 B.C., I took that step.

I was a young palace official when I heard the emperor was looking for someone to travel west through enemy territory to central Asia.

The emperor needed someone to persuade the Scythian tribes of central Asia to help us fight our common foe, the Huns. These Huns lived to the north and west of China.

INTO THE UNKNOWN

Eagerly I applied for the post — and was chosen to lead the expedition!

In 138 B.C., I left the emperor's palace at Xi'an with 100 men and many horses and camels. But no sooner had we entered the Huns' lands than we were taken captive.

I'm sure our enemies would never have let us go, but after 10 long years a number of us escaped, along with our animals.

We struggled across harsh mountain passes into central Asia, and at last reached the Scythians. But to my dismay, I found that I couldn't convince them to help China against the Huns. So at Samarkand I made the decision to turn back.

However, my journey was not in vain. I was the first of my people to travel west of China, and there I learned of the rich civilizations of Rome and India — unknown before back home. I realized that trade with these distant lands could make us rich.

As soon as I returned safely to Xi'an in 126 B.C., I began planning another trip west, this time with gifts of gold and silk.

I am sure that my next journey will open a gateway between China and the rest of the world.

CENTRAL ASIA Chang Chi'en held captive for 10 years

Samarkand 127 B.C. **CHINA** **Xi'an** 138 B.C.

GO WEST: Chang Chi'en's route through central Asia.

SILK ROAD

Chang Chi'en's travels laid the foundation for one of the most famous routes of all time — the Silk Road.

The Silk Road was not a single road. It was the name for all the trading routes that carried silk from China into Europe. The Silk Road was used from about 100 B.C. until well into the A.D. 1300s.

The whole route was 5,000 miles long, from Xi'an in China to Roman ports such as Venice on the Mediterranean Sea.

But traders did not travel the full length of the road, only to the next trading point. There they exchanged goods with merchants from other lands, and then returned home.

DIZZYING HEIGHTS: Chang Chi'en's expedition struggles through snowy mountain passes in central Asia.

AGAINST ALL ODDS: Eriksson and his brave crew battle through icy northern seas in search of new lands.

ERIKSSON'S NEW LAND

Illustrated by GEOFF HUNT

DID THE VIKINGS go too far? *The History News* asked this question in A.D. 1007, after the Vikings left their new country, America — so bravely discovered by explorer Leif Eriksson.

NEWS HAS just reached us that the Vikings, those formidable warriors from Scandinavia, have been forced to flee their new settlement in the West.

It was six years ago when Leif Eriksson, one of the most skillful and daring of all the Viking seafarers, first discovered America, a promising new land to settle.

At the time, this took nobody by surprise. The Vikings are a bold, hardy people who have become known for raiding and settling the lands around them. And they'd already claimed the vast empty island of Greenland to their west.

In fact, it was from Greenland that Eriksson had first set out, back in A.D. 1001. On his return, a year later, he described how he and his crew had sailed through storm-tossed seas, littered with towering icebergs, until at last they had sighted land. Then they'd turned to the south, along the coastline, and had made three landings.

The first was a barren place of ice and rock. At the second, vast forests crowded so thickly near the shore that they could not enter them.

But their third landing had brought them to a rich fertile place that Eriksson named Vinland, after the vines that grew there.

Spurred by Eriksson's description of Vinland, a group of Viking settlers left Greenland in A.D. 1005 to try to live in this new territory.

A couple of years passed well, but then the Vikings started fighting the original inhabitants. And, what's more, these fierce warriors were ready to die for their homeland. For once, it was the Vikings who were driven away.

The fearsome Vikings have long been a force to be reckoned with, but maybe this defeat marks a turn in the tide of Viking success. Perhaps the "wolves of the sea" have met their match! ✴

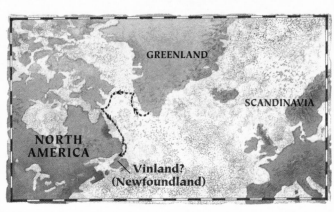

NEW LAND: Eriksson's route to North America.

A MAN OF THE WORLD

Illustrated by VANESSA CARD

AVID TRAVELER Ibn Battuta finally came home in September 1353. Though hard at work on an account of his voyages, he found the time to tell *The History News* about some of his adventures.

My journey started in 1325 when I left Morocco on a pilgrimage to the sacred city of Mecca. That was when I was only 21 years old. Then a holy man told me I should visit China and India. This was all I needed — I was bitten by the travel bug.

1326

Over the next five years, I visited as many holy places in the Middle East as I could, including the city of Jerusalem. I made myself a promise never to travel by the same route twice.

At one point I joined those feared warriors of central Asia, the Mongols. But with their thousands of people, wagons and horses, they traveled so slowly we covered only 5 miles a day.

1332

The farthest north I ventured was into Russia. It was so cold there that the water froze in my beard when I washed my face. And I was so fat with layers of clothing that I could barely walk.

For eight years I worked for the ruler of India. This mad sultan was so vicious that each day he would kill one or two of those who were closest to him. I lived in fear for my life.

1344

One of the richest and most fertile places I visited was China. Here, I watched the finest silks in the world being made. I was amazed to see that instead of gold and silver coins, the Chinese use pieces of paper stamped with the sultan's mark for money.

1350

I longed for home and returned in 1350. I took two more short trips — across the Sahara Desert to Mali, and to Spain. But now I have decided to remain here in Morocco. And as I have seen more of the world, its people, and their strange ways of life than any other person alive, I want to record all my adventures.

ALL THE WAY: Ibn Battuta's journeys took him over most of the world.

A WORLD IN THE WEST

Illustrated by PETER VISSCHER and KEVIN TWEDDELL

HERE WE GO: Columbus's three ships set out from Spain.

ONCE THE VIKINGS had left its shores, all knowledge of "a land in the West" was lost. Then in 1492, the Italian explorer Christopher Columbus set sail for Indonesia — but found America instead! A reporter from *The History News* went with him.

AS OUR SHIP, the *Santa Maria*, gradually pulled away from the Spanish port of Palos, all those waving from the shore must have wondered if we would ever return.

We were headed for the Spice Islands of Indonesia. But instead of sailing east around Africa, Columbus wanted to sail west. Nobody had ever sailed so far in this direction and we had no idea what lay before us!

Columbus, too, was unknown. He had come from Italy and somehow persuaded the king and queen of Spain to fund this voyage in return for all the precious spices, such as cinnamon and cloves, that we would bring from Indonesia.

TROUBLE AT SEA

Columbus was full of confidence when we set sail on August 3, 1492. He had a crew of 90 men and three ships — the *Santa Maria*, the *Pinta*, and the *Nina*.

But we hadn't been at sea long before the crew of the *Santa Maria* began to feel uneasy. Columbus had said we would reach land only a few days after leaving Spain. But as the days turned into weeks, the crew's fears increased.

Each day Columbus told his men how far they'd sailed. But I soon learned that each night he wrote down the real, much longer distance in a secret logbook.

But Columbus could do nothing to stop his men counting the days. And, after four long weeks with still no land in sight, I watched in horror as the crew of the *Santa Maria* turned on their captain and demanded that all three ships return to Spain.

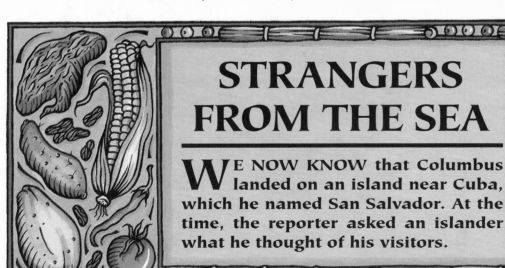

STRANGERS FROM THE SEA

WE NOW KNOW that Columbus landed on an island near Cuba, which he named San Salvador. At the time, the reporter asked an islander what he thought of his visitors.

? **Were you surprised by our arrival?**
I was amazed. I saw your ships coming from the direction of the dawn and I didn't know there was any land that way.

But I was even more shocked when you came ashore. I had never seen people like you before— with pale skin and hairy faces and with your bodies covered in layers of cloth.

? **And how do you feel about us now?**
I feel worried. At first I thought your people

Illustrated by KEVIN TWEDDELL

LAND AHOY! Columbus prepares to take possession of his "New World."

THAT'S NO NEW LAND

COLUMBUS never went to America! At least, that's what he wrote in a letter he sent to *The History News* just before his death in 1506.

> March 23, 1506
>
> Dear Editor,
>
> I have greatly enjoyed your newspaper's many articles in which you have written of all four of my trips across the Atlantic Ocean, between 1492 and 1504. But I must point out one very important error.
>
> In spite of everything that people are saying, I firmly believe that I have not discovered a "New World," as this land is now called. I still say that I reached an island just off the coast of Japan.
>
> I hope you will correct this mistake before it becomes commonly accepted.
>
> *Xp̄o Ferens*
>
> **CHRISTOPHER COLUMBUS**

But Columbus argued fiercely to continue. He asked his men to give him three more days. If they hadn't found land by then, he told them, he would hand over all control of the voyage.

For the next three days, all eyes scanned the horizon. Then, at a little after midnight on the third day, the cry we were longing to hear rang out — "Land! Land!"

At daybreak the next day, we rowed ashore. Planting the Spanish flag firmly in the ground, Columbus claimed this "New World" for Spain.

Columbus believes we have reached an island near Japan, but I am not so sure. The people living here are

not as wealthy as we had expected and seem to have no knowledge of Europe at all.

But wherever we are, no one can doubt that Columbus has led us bravely across unknown seas. Thanks to his skill and perseverance we've opened up a new route to the West. ✳

See pages 14–15 for Columbus's route.

just wanted food and water, so we gave you pumpkins, tomatoes, and maize. We couldn't believe you had never seen such foods before.

In return, you gave us beads and bells. But you kept asking about our gold — how

much we had and where it came from. I have come to realize you only want to take our riches.

I can only hope you will all leave soon. But even then the lives of my people will never be the same again. ✳

LIVING TO TELL THE TALE

Illustrated by CHRIS MOLAN

IN SEPTEMBER 1519, five ships set forth for Indonesia, led by the Portuguese explorer Ferdinand Magellan. Three years later only one, the *Victoria,* limped home. A crew member described what happened.

IT WAS ALL a bit of a disaster, really. You see, like Columbus, Captain Magellan thought we could reach Indonesia by sailing west, even though America is in the way!

But Magellan believed he could find a waterway through that land. Then we could continue west to the islands of Indonesia.

STRAIT CUT

We made the familiar trip from Spain to South America without too many problems. But then we headed south, entering uncharted waters.

It took many months to find what Magellan was looking for. But at last, in October 1520, we discovered a strait that cut through South America.

But by this stage we'd already lost two ships. One was wrecked before we got to the strait. Another turned back to Spain — not everyone was ready to give up his life for Magellan's dream.

We were lucky not to lose a third ship in the strait itself. The waters there are the roughest I've ever known.

When we struggled through to the other side, we arrived, thank God, in an ocean of calm water, which Magellan named the Pacific. We were the first Europeans ever to enter this ocean, and Magellan promised we would reach land in a few days. But it was at least three months before we walked on solid ground once more!

I could never face such a trip again. Our food ran out and many died from hunger and disease.

By March 1521, when we reached the Mariana Islands, we'd eaten rats, sawdust, and the leather from the ships' rigging. Finally finding food and water was better than gold.

Our troubles didn't stop there, though. First Magellan got caught up in an island war and was killed. Then we had to leave one of our ships — so many men had died there weren't enough of us left to sail her.

The captain of that ship, Juan del Cano, took command of our last two ships and led us at last to the Spice Islands. There we loaded up with cloves and other valuable spices, then turned for Spain.

We lost another ship on the journey back, but finally, on September 6, 1522, we made it home.

Of the 250 men who'd begun the voyage, all but 18 were dead. As for Magellan, who will ever remember what he did? After all, we were the ones who sailed around the world, not him! ✳

See pages 14–15 for Magellan's route.

RAT CATCHERS: After months at sea, Magellan's sailors will eat anything.

From *The History News,* 1522

DO-IT-YOURSELF TRIP

Illustrated by CAROLINE CHURCH

AFTER MAGELLAN'S STORY came out in 1522, *The History News* published this useful practical guide for budding explorers in the hope that more of them would survive the dangers at sea.

1 GET SHIPSHAPE!
First you'll need the right ship. A good choice is a Caravela Rodonda — its combination of sails makes it the most popular ship around. The square sails catch the winds on the open sea, making it very fast. The lateen sail means it's easy to steer around the coast.

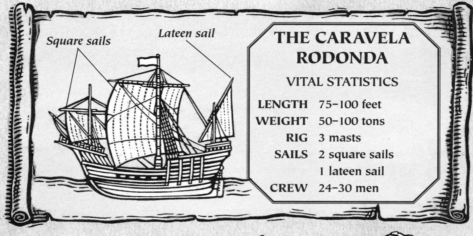

Square sails   Lateen sail

THE CARAVELA RODONDA
VITAL STATISTICS

LENGTH	75–100 feet
WEIGHT	50–100 tons
RIG	3 masts
SAILS	2 square sails
	1 lateen sail
CREW	24–30 men

Another vital item is a log line. It's easy to use — just throw the log overboard, keeping firm hold of the knotted line attached to it. Then use an hourglass to count the number of knots that pass through your hands in a certain amount of time. This will help you roughly guess your speed.

ALL ABOARD: Pick crew members who can turn their hands to many tasks.

GO WITH THE FLOW: Check speed with a log line.

UP AND UP: Only recruit fit and healthy crews.

2 HANDS ON DECK
It can be hard to get a good crew. Magellan had to hire prisoners who were given their freedom if they agreed to go on his voyage!

Your crew will have to be prepared to work hard — adjusting the sails each time the wind changes, manning the lookout post 24 hours a day, and keeping the deck scrubbed. But don't bother to hire a cook — each crew member can take turns preparing a daily meal on deck.

3 FOOD 'N' DRINK
Once you have a crew, you can figure out what supplies you will need. The basics are fish and bacon — salted so they don't go bad — flour, for making bread, cheese, oil, salt, and hard biscuits. You'll also need vast amounts of drinking water. But it won't stay fresh for long, so take plenty of wine and beer, as well.

Pack some mirrors, glass beads, bells, and brightly colored cloth, too. When you reach land you can trade them for more food supplies.

4 WHERE ARE WE?
You'll need sea charts, of course, to figure out your position each day. And take a compass so you can make sure you're sailing in the right direction.

5 WHAT ELSE?
Don't forget all the other essentials — hammocks for the crew, hooks and lines so they can catch fresh fish, pots and pans, firewood for cooking meals, and oil lanterns for lighting below deck.

Be sure to take lots of weapons, too. You never know who you'll meet.

Good luck!

MAGELLAN'S VOYAGE AROUND THE WORLD IN THE 1500S MADE PEOPLE QUESTION IDEAS THAT HAD BEEN HELD FOR CENTURIES. ANCIENT MAPS OF THE LANDS AND THE OCEANS NO LONGER SEEMED TO MAKE SENSE.

EVEN BELIEFS ABOUT THE SHAPE OF OUR WORLD WERE TURNED UPSIDE DOWN. AT THE TIME, *THE HISTORY NEWS* WAS ONE OF THE FIRST TO EXAMINE THE EVIDENCE — AND ARGUE FOR A NEW WAY OF THINKING.

JUNK THIS MAP

Illustrated by GILLIAN TYLER

MAGELLAN'S VOYAGE proved what many explorers had known for some time — the most famous map in the world, the Ptolemaic map, was utterly wrong! In 1522, *The History News* revealed five errors that showed it was time to change our view of the world.

1 IT'S OLD NEWS

This map is based on the works of Ptolemy, a Greek scholar who lived between A.D. 127 and 147. He created a grid for his map and listed the grid positions of about 8,000 places.

The map was the most detailed chart of its time, and it was copied for many centuries — first by Arabic scholars, and since 1406 by European mapmakers.

But we say it's time to have another look! Ptolemy wrote down his ideas nearly 1,400 years ago. And back in those days there was simply no way of accurately measuring distance. So, many of the grid positions Ptolemy recorded are wrong.

2 AFRICA ENDS

On the Ptolemaic map, Africa is joined to a huge land called the Unknown Continent.

Yet back in 1488, a Portuguese sailor named Bartholomeu Dias proved that Africa did end, when he sailed to the southern tip of Africa — known as the Cape of Good Hope.

3 AMERICA'S OFF THE MAP

Then there's Columbus's journey in 1492. He had examined the Ptolemaic map and was sure that he would reach Asia if he sailed west from Europe.

So he did — only to find America where Asia should have been. The Ptolemaic map shows no sign of either North or South America.

MAD MAP: Is the Ptolemaic map, as shown in this version published in 1482, really a true picture of the world we know?

4 OCEAN'S NOT LANDLOCKED

The map also shows the Indian Ocean completely surrounded by land. But in 1498, a Portuguese sailor named Vasco da Gama proved that wrong.

He sailed all the way around the Cape of Good Hope and then across the Indian Ocean to the coast of India. According to Ptolemy, such a trip would not be possible.

5 THE WORLD'S A BIG PLACE

Not only did Ptolemy get the position of many places wrong, he got the whole world wrong!

Ptolemy thought Earth was much smaller than it actually is. In fact, he believed that the earth was only roughly two-thirds the size it is.

No wonder Magellan believed he would reach land just a few days after sailing through the tip of South America and entering the Pacific Ocean. Instead it took him more than three months, and much of his crew starved.

The History News says it's time to correct these errors and put Ptolemy's map in a museum. ✳

See pages 14–15 for all the routes mentioned.

THE REAL WORLD

IN THIS MODERN AGE, all corners of the earth have been mapped. Satellites even take pictures of the world from space so there can be no doubt about the size and shape of our lands. Today's map shows just how incomplete the Ptolemaic map was.

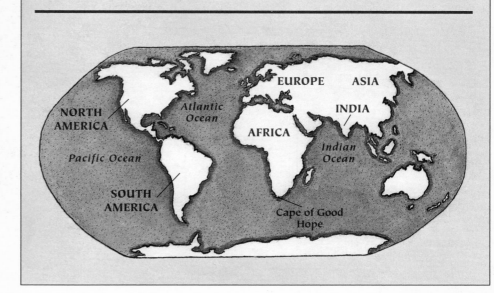

NORTH AMERICA · EUROPE · ASIA · INDIA · Atlantic Ocean · AFRICA · Pacific Ocean · Indian Ocean · SOUTH AMERICA · Cape of Good Hope

A FLAT DENIAL

AFTER 1522, there could be no doubt that the earth was round. Yet there were still those who clung to the idea that the world was flat. This letter, sent to *The History News* in 1523, shows how some people felt.

Dear Editor,

Have you gone raving mad? I ask this question after reading a recent article in your paper in which you describe the world as round.

If it were so, I would surely topple over on the curved surface, which is certainly not the case.

A paper so highly respected as *The History News* simply can't afford to make such a basic mistake. I look forward to seeing a correction in a future issue.

Yours,
An Angry Reader

Our Science Editor replies:

Sir, you are correct. We cannot afford to make mistakes, which is why we say in our paper that the world is a globe.

The idea was first put forward in the 400s B.C., by a Greek thinker named Pythagoras. He observed that when a lunar eclipse occurs, the earth blocks the sun's light from the moon and you can see the earth's shadow pass across the moon. The curved shadow shows that Earth is round.

The Arabs have long known of this theory, of course, although it was only rediscovered by Europeans in the 1100s.

But let us consider what would happen if Earth really were flat. It would have to end somewhere — in which case, Magellan's ships would have sailed off the edge! Instead, one ship returned to Spain, having sailed around the world. This proves what most people believe already — our world is round. ✳

AARGH!

THE EDGE OF THE WORLD

Cartoon by TONY KENYON

THE WORLD — MAJOR

Illustrated by DAVID ATKINSON

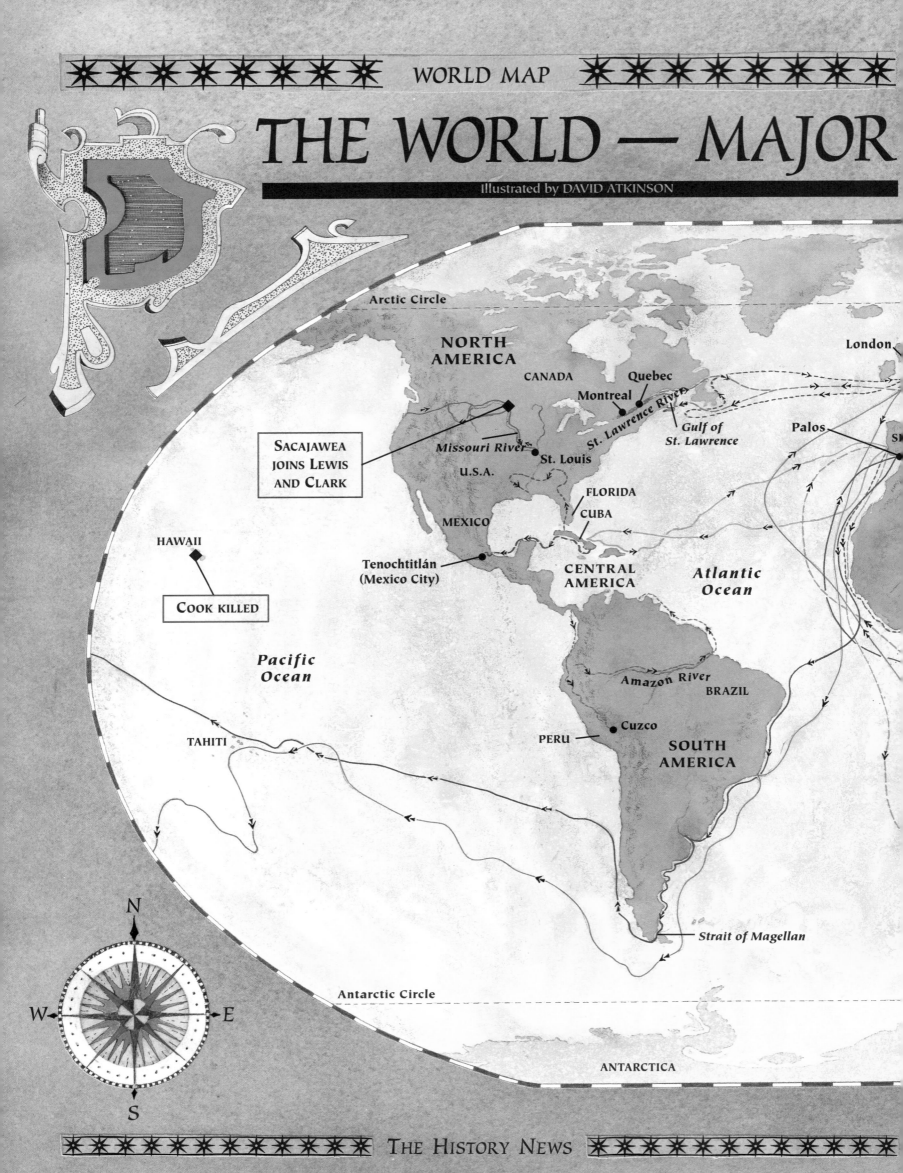

Arctic Circle

NORTH
AMERICA

CANADA

Quebec

Montreal

St. Lawrence River

Gulf of
St. Lawrence

London

Palos

SACAJAWEA
JOINS LEWIS
AND CLARK

Missouri River

St. Louis

U.S.A.

FLORIDA

CUBA

MEXICO

HAWAII

Tenochtitlán
(Mexico City)

CENTRAL
AMERICA

Atlantic
Ocean

COOK KILLED

Pacific
Ocean

Amazon River

BRAZIL

TAHITI

Cuzco

PERU

SOUTH
AMERICA

Strait of Magellan

N

Antarctic Circle

W

E

ANTARCTICA

S

EXPLORERS' ROUTES

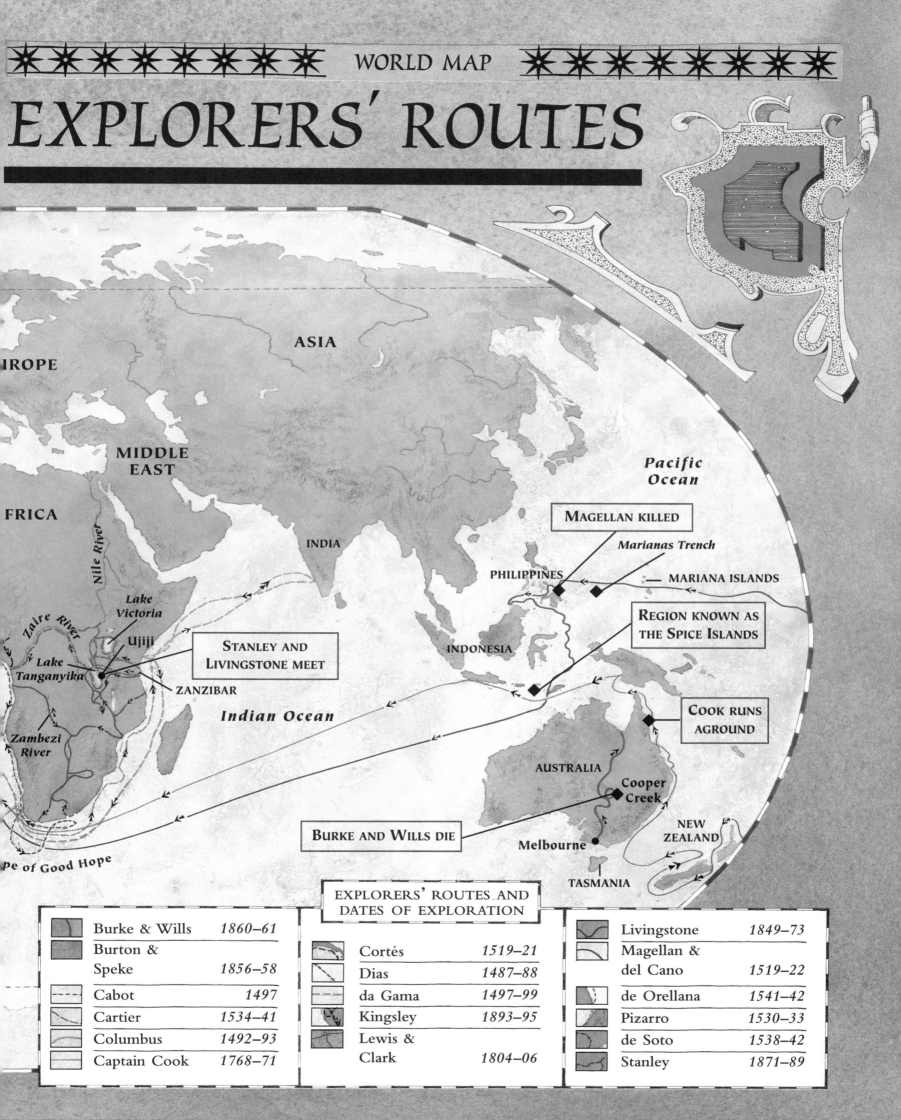

ASIA

EUROPE

MIDDLE EAST

AFRICA

Nile River

Pacific Ocean

INDIA

MAGELLAN KILLED

Marianas Trench

PHILIPPINES — MARIANA ISLANDS

Lake Victoria

Zaire River

Ujiji

REGION KNOWN AS THE SPICE ISLANDS

Lake Tanganyika

STANLEY AND LIVINGSTONE MEET

INDONESIA

ZANZIBAR

Indian Ocean

COOK RUNS AGROUND

Zambezi River

AUSTRALIA

Cooper Creek

BURKE AND WILLS DIE

NEW ZEALAND

Melbourne

Cape of Good Hope

TASMANIA

EXPLORERS' ROUTES AND DATES OF EXPLORATION

Burke & Wills		1860–61
Burton & Speke		1856–58
Cabot		1497
Cartier		1534–41
Columbus		1492–93
Captain Cook		1768–71

Cortés		1519–21
Dias		1487–88
da Gama		1497–99
Kingsley		1893–95
Lewis & Clark		1804–06

Livingstone		1849–73
Magellan & del Cano		1519–22
de Orellana		1541–42
Pizarro		1530–33
de Soto		1538–42
Stanley		1871–89

SPANISH HERO DIES

Illustrated by RICHARD BERRIDGE

A DEADLY ENCOUNTER: Aztec weapons are no match for the metal armor and swords of the Spanish soldiers.

THE FLOOD of Europeans to the mainland of America began with a conquest by the famous Spanish adventurer Hernán Cortés. After his death in 1547, *The History News* paid him this tribute.

HERNÁN CORTÉS, aged 62 years, has died at his home near Seville in southern Spain. He will be remembered as a courageous soldier, an inspiring leader, and the conqueror of the mighty Aztec empire in Mexico and Central America.

Cortés was born in Spain in 1485. In 1504, at the age of 19, he gave up his studies in law and set off to seek his fortune in the New World.

For the next 14 years, Cortés helped to govern the Spanish-held islands that lay near the coast of Central America, and he took part in the Spanish conquest of Cuba. Then, in 1518, came the chance he'd been waiting for.

Cortés persuaded the governor of Cuba to let him investigate rumors that Mexico was ruled by a people rich in gold.

FOR GOLD AND GLORY

With an army of about 500 men, 16 horses, and some cannons, Cortés set sail for the Mexican coast in November 1518.

He first landed at the settlement of Tabasco, where the people were so terrified at the sight of guns and horses, having seen neither before, that the Spaniards had no difficulty defeating them.

From these people, Cortés learned that much of Mexico was ruled by a powerful and rich tribe called the Aztecs. His dreams of glory and gold seemed within reach.

Cortés moved farther along the coast and set up camp at a place he called Veracruz. He then marched his army inland, toward the Aztec capital of Tenochtitlán.

He reached the city in November 1519, having enlarged his force with tribes who were bitter enemies of the Aztecs.

At first, the Aztecs let the strangers into their capital. But then Cortés took their ruler hostage. And when the Spaniards turned to slaughter, the Aztecs rebelled.

A long and vicious war followed. But by 1521, Cortés had crushed the Aztec empire and claimed Mexico for Spain.

Aztec wealth poured out of Mexico, tempting many Spanish adventurers to go there. Cortés was a hero in his country.

But although honors were heaped upon him, Cortés was never given the power in Mexico that he felt he deserved. He returned to Spain in 1540 to die a disappointed and forgotten man.

Yet despite his sorry end, here at *The History News* we have little doubt that Cortés's exploits will long be remembered in times to come.

WHAT ABOUT THE NORTH?

Illustrated by CHRIS MOLAN

WHILE SPAIN dominated the southern parts of the Americas, France was doing its best to open up the interior of the far north. *The History News* spoke to the French explorer Jacques Cartier in 1550.

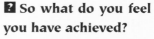

RAPID RIDE: Native Americans help Cartier on a rough river.

❓ How many trips did you make to Canada?
I led three expeditions in all, in 1534, 1535, and also in 1541. I was seeking a river route through North America to the Pacific Ocean, and from there to Indonesia. To tell you the truth, I doubt now that a route exists.

❓ Was yours the first European expedition to sail to the far north?
No, not at all. There were a few others before me. I believe the first was the English expedition led by John Cabot, which arrived in 1497. But all of them sailed along the coast. None went inland.

❓ And you did?
Absolutely! On my first two expeditions, I not only explored the vast Gulf of St. Lawrence, but sailed 1,000 miles up the St. Lawrence River, as far as the point I have named Mount Royal. No other explorer has ever traveled this far inland.

We would have gone farther if we could, but sadly the river ahead was blocked by rapids.

❓ Did you ever think of staying in Canada?
Yes. On my third trip, in 1541, we tried to build a settlement in Quebec. But we had to abandon it after only one winter — the climate was so harsh!

❓ So what do you feel you have achieved?
I am most proud of the friendly relationships I have built up with the local people.

For example, they have often helped me on my explorations. And I have been able to set up a valuable trade in furs, exchanging them for our metal knives and axes.

My hope is that other Frenchmen will return to settle in Canada one day, perhaps using the base I started in Quebec.

❓ And will you return to Canada yourself?
Oh, no. I intend to remain in France now, to write about my adventures. ✷

FAIR SWAP: Cartier and the local people meet at villages like Quebec to trade.

BY THE LATE 1700S, EXPLORATION WASN'T SIMPLY A QUESTION OF SEARCHING FOR UNKNOWN LANDS. IT WAS ALSO ABOUT MAPPING THEM, MEASURING THEM, AND STUDYING THEM IN DETAIL — THE AGE OF SCIENTIFIC EXPLORATION HAD BEGUN. ONE OF THE FIRST, AND SURELY ONE OF THE GREATEST, OF THESE EARLY SCIENTIFIC EXPEDITIONS WAS THE VOYAGE OF THE ENGLISHMAN CAPTAIN JAMES COOK TO THE PACIFIC OCEAN.

Captain Cook in his cabin

A STRANGE CHOICE?

Illustrated by PETER VISSCHER

IN 1771, a British naval expedition returned home from exploring the Pacific Ocean. At the time, critics said that its leader, Captain James Cook, should never have been sent. *The History News* found out what all the fuss was about.

CAPTAIN COOK has gone home to London after a voyage lasting three years. The coasts of Australia and New Zealand, unknown before, are now mapped. And the many scientists with him have thoroughly explored these countries, returning with strange new animals and plants. Surely, the trip has been a great success. Yet not everyone agrees. Here, we give three points of view.

A CRITIC

I can't understand why Cook was chosen to lead this expedition. He didn't join the navy until he was at least 27 years old, and then he started as just an ordinary seaman. It's unheard of for someone at the bottom to work his way up through the ranks like this.

And look at the ship he chose for this trip. The *Endeavour* is just a shabby coal boat. Is this how we want the British navy to be represented? That man Cook should have been satisfied working for a coal merchant, not have joined the Royal Navy!

ONE OF THE SCIENTISTS

Cook was chosen as our captain because he is a good leader and a very fine navigator. You only need to look at the remarkably accurate maps he made when he was sent to explore the coastline of Canada. It's no wonder the navy selected him for this important trip.

Cook was right in his choice of ship, too. The *Endeavour* was designed to carry a lot of cargo, so we had plenty of room for supplies. We even had space to build cabins for our scientific studies.

And as the *Endeavour* is a shallow ship, we could sail quite a long way up rivers and were able to explore inland.

The boat even saved our lives. We ran aground just off the Australian

LANDS IN THE SEA

BEFORE COOK'S expedition, most of the vast Pacific Ocean and its many islands were a mystery to the western world. But by 1779, the area was firmly on the map.

1605: Dutch ships land in northern Australia. The sailors keep their find a secret and don't mark it on any maps.

1642 & 1644: A Dutch sea captain named Abel Tasman charts a few areas of Tasmania, New Zealand, Fiji, and the north coast of Australia.

1768: Maps show only a few scattered Pacific islands, the north coast of Australia, and a small fragment of the coast of New Zealand. Nobody knows how big these last two lands are, or if they are connected.

1768–71: On his first voyage, Cook charts the east coast of Australia and maps both main islands of New Zealand, proving that they are all separate islands. He also locates and maps many other Pacific islands.

1772–75: Cook's next journey to the Pacific Ocean takes him to the icy waters of the far south, where no one has ever been before. He sails right around the continent of Antarctica.

1776–79: Cook's third trip is to the northern Pacific Ocean. There he explores the west coast of North America, trying, without success, to find a way through to the Atlantic Ocean. ✳

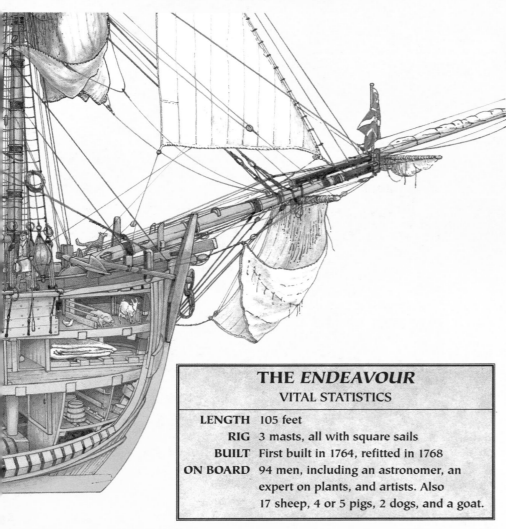

THE *ENDEAVOUR*
VITAL STATISTICS

LENGTH	105 feet
RIG	3 masts, all with square sails
BUILT	First built in 1764, refitted in 1768
ON BOARD	94 men, including an astronomer, an expert on plants, and artists. Also 17 sheep, 4 or 5 pigs, 2 dogs, and a goat.

coast and escaped only by throwing all the food stores, even our drinking water, overboard. The boat was able to float free — a deeper ship would have been stuck for good.

ONE OF THE CREW

I'll say this for Captain Cook, he takes care of his men. Unlike most other officers, he's lived below the decks himself, so he knows what it's like.

He's got a real bee in his bonnet about health and keeping things clean. We had to open the hatches to air the lower decks each day. And every three days he'd tell us to shake out our clothing and bedding. He even made us scrub the ship from top to bottom with vinegar every week.

He had some strange ideas about food, too. As well as the usual ship's biscuits and beer, we ate fresh vegetables, pickled cabbage, and lemon juice. We complained about it, but the captain was eating the very same food.

He knew what he was doing, though. Not one of us got scurvy and that's a miracle on a long voyage. Scurvy kills more sailors than enemy gunshot.

The captain's a great man. All those who think otherwise should sail with him. They'll soon change their mind! ✳

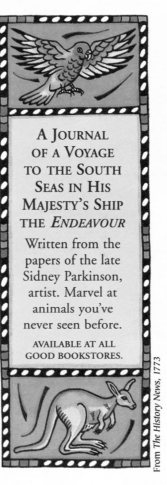

A JOURNAL OF A VOYAGE TO THE SOUTH SEAS IN HIS MAJESTY'S SHIP THE *ENDEAVOUR*

Written from the papers of the late Sidney Parkinson, artist. Marvel at animals you've never seen before.

AVAILABLE AT ALL GOOD BOOKSTORES.

From The History News, 1773

CAPTAIN JAMES COOK
～ 1728–1779 ～

IT IS WITH GREAT SORROW THAT WE ANNOUNCE THE DEATH OF CAPTAIN JAMES COOK. WHILE ON HIS THIRD VOYAGE IN THE PACIFIC OCEAN, CAPTAIN COOK WAS TRAGICALLY KILLED DURING A CONFLICT WITH THE ISLANDERS OF HAWAII. THE WORLD HAS LOST A GREAT EXPLORER.

THE ADMIRALTY, LONDON, ENGLAND

From The History News, 1779

GIRL GUIDE

Illustrated by PETER DENNIS

IN 1804, an expedition set off to explore the western lands of North America. Its success came to depend on a Native American girl, Sacajawea. Here *The History News* celebrates the vital role she played.

SACAJAWEA certainly led a remarkable life. She was born into the Shoshone people in the Midwest of North America, but as a child she was snatched by the Hidatsa tribe.

Sacajawea was taken to the east. Then, at just 17 years old, she joined an expedition that would make her name famous.

The exploration was requested by President Thomas Jefferson. He wanted to investigate the Louisiana Purchase, a huge area of land that his government had just bought from the French.

The land lay west of the Mississippi River. Jefferson's young aide, Meriwether Lewis, was to lead the team, along with an army colleague of his named William Clark.

The party of 47 men

GREETINGS: Sacajawea makes the first contact between Lewis and Clark and the Shoshone.

left St. Louis in May 1804 and headed north along the Missouri River. When winter fell, they settled at a place called Mandan.

Here the explorers found they had to cross land controlled by the Shoshone — a people no European had ever seen.

It was then that they met Sacajawea. When Lewis and Clark learned that this Hidatsa girl was actually a Shoshone, they got the idea of asking her to act as their guide and translator.

For three long months

Sacajawea traveled with Lewis and Clark and their men as they struggled farther upriver. Finally they reached the land she had left as a child — Shoshone land.

HORSE TRADING

Sacajawea's help now became crucial to the expedition. She not only convinced her people that Lewis and Clark meant no harm, but she helped to persuade the tribe's chief to sell the expedition the

horses they needed to continue their journey.

With Sacajawea in the lead, the party now rode into the towering Rocky Mountains, looking for a safe route through. After weeks of searching, they finally found a river that flowed west. Eagerly they followed it until, on November 15, 1805, they reached the shore of the Pacific Ocean — the first expedition ever to cross to the west of America.

The journey ended in great success — thanks to the skills of Sacajawea! ✳

TRAGEDY IN OUTBACK

Illustrated by CHRIS COLLINGWOOD

IN 1860 A PRIZE OF $3,000 was offered to anyone who could cross Australia from coast to coast. But instead of riches, the first men across found only tragedy.

THE EXPEDITION that set off from Melbourne in southern Australia on August 20, 1860, had been planned with great precision.

Every last detail had been thought of — except for one thing. The man chosen to be the leader, Robert Burke, had little experience of exploration. How would he cope with a trek of almost 1,900 miles?

Burke was a very willful, impulsive man, too, not fit to handle a team of 15 men, 23 horses, and 27 camels. These failings would prove to be fatal.

By the time the party reached Cooper Creek, 870 miles to the north, Burke had become impatient with their slow progress. He ordered his foreman, William Brahe, to stay with the rest of the team at Cooper Creek for three months. Then Burke set off for the coast, along with William Wills, Charles Gray, and John King.

At first, the four men made good speed. Then the rainy season began, and the ground became too waterlogged for the pack animals. Burke left them with King and Gray, and he and Wills decided to carry on alone.

By the middle of February 1861, the two men finally arrived at the north coast. They heard waves crashing on the shore, but they could not reach the sea. They'd exhausted themselves by trying to fight through the swampy land.

They returned to King and Gray and began the long trek back. But all four were weakened by hunger and illness, and on April 17, Gray died.

Four days later, after 18 long weeks away, the three survivors crawled into Cooper Creek. To their horror they found it deserted. Brahe and the others had left for Melbourne only a few hours before!

AT DEATH'S DOOR

Burke, Wills, and King set off to find help, but soon became hopelessly lost.

On September 18, 1861, King was found, half dead, by a search party. He had survived on food given to him by a group of local Aborigines.

Unfortunately for Burke and Wills, the success of being first to cross the continent had turned to tragedy long before.

By the end of June 1861, both men lay dead. ✳

A GRUELING HIKE: Burke, Wills, and King struggle to return to their camp at Cooper Creek. They think they will reach safety — but their problems are just beginning.

Although Africa's coastline had been mapped by the beginning of the 1800s, it was still largely a place of legend to the Western world. Then, in an effort both to explore the interior and to open up new opportunites for trade, expedition after expedition went there. *The History News* highlights some of the intrepid men and women who journeyed deep into the heart of Africa.

FOUR OF THE BEST

Illustrated by CHRIS MOLAN

ASK ANYONE to list their top ten explorers of Africa and these names are certain to appear. *The History News* **takes a look at their greatest achievements.**

1 JOHN HANNING SPEKE

To explorers, one of the chief mysteries of Africa was the Nile River. Many had set out to discover where it began, but when they traveled up the river it seemed to vanish into swampy marshes.

In 1856 two British army officers, Speke and Richard Burton, resolved to explore some inland lakes they had heard of, which they hoped might be the source of the Nile.

After a year's traveling inland from the coast of east Africa, they found a large lake called Lake Tanganyika. Once there, they realized from its position that it could not be the Nile's source.

Burton became ill, but Speke continued on to a lake in the north that he called Lake Victoria. There he boldly claimed it was the source of the Nile — and was proved right by Henry Stanley in 1874.

2 DAVID LIVINGSTONE

Livingstone is known as the greatest explorer of Africa. He arrived first as a missionary in 1841, but in 1853 he devoted his life to exploration.

He spent the next 20 years traveling deep into the continent. He was the first explorer to cross southern Africa, first to discover the thunderous Victoria Falls, and first to explore and travel up the vast Zambezi River.

3 HENRY MORTON STANLEY

Stanley was bitten by the exploring bug in 1871, when he led an expedition in search of Dr. Livingstone, whom many thought was dead.

THE SEARCH IS ON: Speke and Burton seek to solve the riddle of the Nile River.

In 1874, he traveled to Lake Victoria and there confirmed Speke's belief that it was the source of the Nile River. His many other expeditions included five years spent around the Zaire River, the last major river in Africa to be explored.

4 MARY KINGSLEY

Kingsley, who made two trips to the north of the Zaire River between 1893 and 1895, was unusual for an explorer. First, she was a woman, at a time when most explorers were men. Second, she was not interested in using a large team of porters. She traveled on her own with just a few guides.

Finally, her aim was not just to explore. She was also dedicated to becoming an expert on the life and religions of the areas she visited. ✴

PLEASED TO MEET YOU: Stanley greets Dr. Livingstone, the man many thought was dead.

LIVINGSTONE ALIVE!

Illustrated by ANGUS McBRIDE

STANLEY'S QUEST to track down Livingstone was one of the most celebrated of all the expeditions in Africa. In 1871, *The History News* spoke to one of the guides who went with him — Sidi Moobarik Bombay.

I FIRST MET up with the American Henry Stanley on the day he arrived in the town of Zanzibar, on the coast of east Africa. It was January 26, 1871.

He wanted to find the great explorer Dr. David Livingstone. Stanley told us how this man was a legend in Europe and America and how people there followed his every adventure. But apparently there had been no news of Livingstone for three years, and many people believed he was dead. Stanley declared he was out to prove these people wrong. He kept boasting of how he'd been sent by a famous newspaper, *The New York Herald*, with one single instruction — find Dr. Livingstone!

Stanley asked me to help organize his trip. It was one of the biggest I'd ever seen. He had to hire 200 porters to carry all his equipment.

Mind you, money was no problem — Stanley had been told he could spend more than $1,500. Most porters are paid about $9 a year, so this amount seemed like a fortune!

Dr. Livingstone had last been last heard of at a place called Ujiji, near Lake Tanganyika. I'd already traveled there with other expeditions, so I knew the route well.

We left Zanzibar on March 21, 1871, and for seven months we fought our way through hostile lands filled with warring tribes and disease.

Finally, on October 30 we reached Ujiji. And there we found a pale, sick-looking man in a battered old blue suit.

Stanley removed his hat and greeted him, "Dr. Livingstone, I presume?" and opened a bottle of champagne he'd carried all that way with him.

LOST AND FOUND

At last, the mystery was solved. The man they call the greatest explorer of Africa had been found, safe and sound.

I'm told this story was important news in other far-off countries, and it makes me proud to think that I was present at this historic meeting. ❋

SIDI MOOBARIK BOMBAY

Although he started life as a slave, Sidi Moobarik Bombay rose to riches as a leader and guide for many European explorers.

1857–58: He traveled with Burton and Speke when they journeyed to Lake Tanganyika.

1860–63: He joined Speke again, this time with James Grant, on a trip to Lake Victoria.

1871–72: He helped Stanley's expedition to find Livingstone.

1873–75: He was with the explorer Verney Lovett Cameron when he crossed Africa from east to west.

1876: Bombay retired in comfort after all his travels, living on the pensions granted to him by the Royal Geographical Society in Great Britain.

By the 1900s, most of the countries of the world were known and mapped. There were few places left to "discover." Instead, explorers were driven by a desire to conquer the world's last frontiers. People raced to be the first to reach the North and South Poles and to explore the oceans' depths. *The History News* applauds those who traveled to the ends of the earth.

PEARY'S AT POLE!

Illustrated by STEVE NOON

SNOW STORMING: Peary battles against blizzards to reach the North Pole.

ON APRIL 6, 1909, the American explorer Robert Peary stood at the very top of the world — the North Pole. *The History News* looks back at Peary's Arctic exploration and at the bitter debate that followed.

PEARY ALWAYS wanted to be a famous explorer. Ever since he was a child, he had been fascinated by the Arctic, and he was determined to uncover its secrets and conquer this dangerous and icy land.

In 1886, at the age of 30, Peary made the first of seven visits inside the Arctic Circle. He believed the best way to survive was to copy how the Inuit people in Greenland lived. So he wore Inuit clothes and ate the same foods as the Inuits. And he learned from them how to keep warm in the freezing cold, how to make a raft out of chunks of ice, and how to use dogs to pull sleds.

He put these methods to the test with two early attempts at the North Pole, but was driven back by storms and dangerous shifting ice. By 1908, he was ready for his third assault on his goal.

THE NORTHWEST PASSAGE

OUR "ARMCHAIR EXPLORER" column has long been popular with readers. Here we answer a query about the Northwest Passage.

❓ Just what is the Northwest Passage — and why are people so interested in it?
It's the channel of ice and water at the top of North America that joins the Pacific and Atlantic Oceans. At one time, people hoped it might prove to be another sea route to Indonesia and so to the Spice Islands.

In the 1500s, routes to the East around Africa or South America were controlled by Portugal and Spain. So other nations, such as France and England, thought they would try to sail through the Northwest Passage, even though nobody then knew if the channel led as far as the Pacific Ocean.

Over the next 350 years there were at least 80 expeditions —

All through the long dark winter, Inuit women sewed clothes and boots for his team, while the men hunted caribou and bear to make stores of smoked meat.

By February 20, 1909, everything was ready. Advance parties led by expert Inuits left to open a trail. Other groups were sent to set up supply bases along the route. Finally, on March 1, Peary set off with 26 men, 133 dogs, and 19 sleds.

Progress was slow. Time and again, the men had to haul the sleds over ridges of ice as high as 50 feet. The party struggled to cover even 11 miles a day.

THE HOME STRAIGHT

However, Peary's planning paid off. On the morning of April 2, 1909, Peary gathered a small team for the last dash to the Pole. He was accompanied by four Inuits, five sleds,

38 husky dogs, and his butler, a black man named Matthew Henson, who had traveled with Peary on every expedition for the last 23 years.

Five days later, after tough forced marches, the men stood on the top of the world. "The Pole at last," Peary wrote in his diary. "Mine. . . ."

But was it?

On the way home, Peary stopped at a port in Labrador. What he heard there astonished him.

A man named Frederick Cook, a doctor who had once traveled with Peary 17 years before, was saying that he had beaten Peary to the Pole, by a year!

Who was the world to believe — Cook or Peary?

Cook failed to produce any records to back up his claim. He said that he had given his notes to some Americans he had met on the way home, for

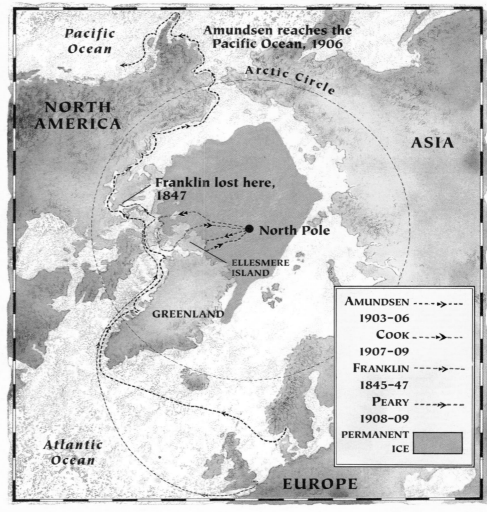

Amundsen reaches the Pacific Ocean, 1906

Arctic Circle

Pacific Ocean

NORTH AMERICA

ASIA

Franklin lost here, 1847

● **North Pole**

← **ELLESMERE ISLAND**

GREENLAND

Atlantic Ocean

EUROPE

| AMUNDSEN ----▶--- |
| 1903–06 |
| COOK ----▶--- |
| 1907–09 |
| FRANKLIN ----▶--- |
| 1845–47 |
| PEARY ----▶--- |
| 1908–09 |
| PERMANENT ICE ☐ |

ON TOP: Both the North Pole and the Northwest Passage were conquered in the 1900s.

safekeeping. But these notes were never seen again. And even the two Inuits who had traveled with him denied they had been at the North Pole.

Peary, on the other

hand, had witnesses to back up his claim and a record of his expedition.

The conflict raged on until finally, in 1911, the rival claims were debated by the United States

Congress. The vote was 135 to 34 — for Peary.

Peary was triumphant at last. As he had written in his diary all those years ago, "My life's work is completed." ✳

all of them failures! Then, in 1845, a British explorer, John Franklin, sailed deep into the passage. But his boat got stuck in the ice and he never returned.

Search parties out looking for him were the first to realize that

the channel went right through. But their boats weren't strong enough to sail the whole way.

The first person to do this was a Norwegian explorer named Roald Amundsen, in a steamship. It took him three years, but in 1906 he arrived in the Pacific Ocean, having sailed all the way through the Northwest Passage. ✳

AMUNDSEN TRIUMPHS

Illustrated by DARREN PATTENDEN

A FAMOUS RACE began in 1910. Norwegian explorer Roald Amundsen and British naval officer Robert Scott were battling it out to be the first to the South Pole. For the next two years, *The History News* tracked their progress through the Antarctic wastes.

BOTH AMUNDSEN and Scott had set sail with their men in June 1910.

Amundsen's mission was simply to be the first to reach the South Pole. Scott, however, wanted to organize a scientific expedition and explore Antarctica. But when Scott heard that Amundsen was coming south, he knew a race was unavoidable.

By January 1911, both men had arrived at Antarctica. Next, advance parties from both teams laid down supply depots along the two separate routes, where they stored food and fuel. This had to be done before the long polar winter began.

By April, the cold and dark had set in, and both teams dug in and waited for the Antarctic spring in September.

READY, SET, GO!

By October, the warmer weather made traveling possible at last, and the teams prepared to set off.

OCTOBER 20, 1911
Amundsen leaves camp on the 800-mile trek to the Pole. His team is made up of just five men on skis, with four sleds, and 52 dogs.

NOVEMBER 1, 1911
Scott's team leaves base camp. The 12-man crew also travels on skis, but there the similarity ends. Scott's sleds are pulled by ten ponies and some dogs. He even takes two motorized tractors, but within just a week, both

TOP DOG: Amundsen reaches the South Pole.

of them break down and are abandoned.

NOVEMBER 17, 1911
Amundsen reaches the steep face of the Trans-Antarctic Mountains. He takes a week to climb a grim 9,840-foot glacier that leads through the mountains. At the top, on the flat Antarctic plateau, his route is easier. He does not need so many dogs now, so he shoots half to feed the rest.

DECEMBER 10, 1911
Scott reaches the Trans-Antarctic Mountains after numerous problems. His ponies had become so exhausted that Scott had shot them. But then the dogs proved difficult to control, so some of his

team took them back to the base. Scott's men now had to pull the sleds themselves.

DECEMBER 14, 1911
Amundsen and his men reach the South Pole, the first people on Earth ever to do so. They raise the Norwegian flag, rest for three days, then begin the journey back.

JANUARY 4, 1912
Scott reaches the top of the glacier at last. The rest of his team returns to base and Scott sets off on a final dash with four others — Lawrence Oates, Edward Wilson, Henry Bowers, and Edgar Evans.

HEAVE HO: Scott and his men battle through the icy Antarctic.

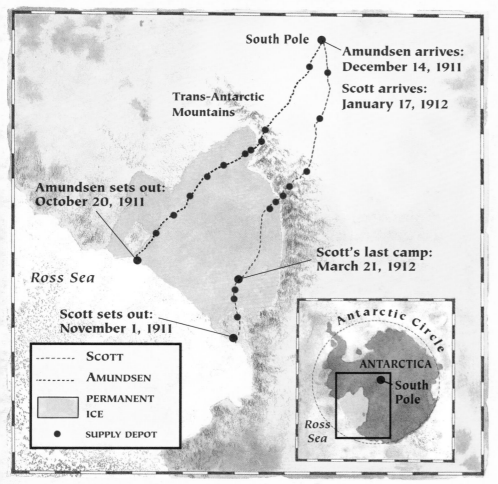

TWO TEAMS, ONE GOAL: Amundsen and Scott race across the Antarctic.

South Pole

Amundsen arrives:
December 14, 1911

Scott arrives:
January 17, 1912

Trans-Antarctic
Mountains

Amundsen sets out:
October 20, 1911

Scott's last camp:
March 21, 1912

Ross Sea

Scott sets out:
November 1, 1911

- - - - - SCOTT
· · · · · AMUNDSEN
☐ PERMANENT ICE
● SUPPLY DEPOT

Antarctic Circle
ANTARCTICA
South Pole
Ross Sea

JANUARY 17, 1912

Scott reaches the Pole, but is devastated to see the Norwegian flag flying there already.

JANUARY 25, 1912

Amundsen arrives back at his base camp. A week later he sails for Norway.

Meanwhile, Scott and his team are struggling to return. All five men are weak from lack of food, sickness, and frostbite. Evans falls ill and dies on February 17. On March 16, Oates walks out of the tent and never returns.

MARCH 21, 1912

After a few more days, the three remaining men are stopped by a blizzard. They put up a tent and crawl inside for shelter.

Bowers and Wilson die first and Scott a few days later. Scott's last entry in his logbook is dated March 29, 1912.

Locked in by the arrival of winter once more, it is

months before a search party can leave to look for Scott and his men.

On November 12, 1912, the search party at last finds the three bodies — just 11 miles away from a food supply depot and safety. ✳

BRAVING THE BLIZZARD: Oates walks off to his death.

LETTER TO *THE HISTORY NEWS*, 1912

Dear Editor,
I was interested to read recently that polar explorers often use dogs to pull their sleds. Wouldn't ponies be more efficient?
Yours sincerely,
A Confused Reader

Dear Reader,
In theory, you are right! Scott figured out that a pony eats seven times more food than a dog, but it pulls sixteen times more weight.

But ponies get stuck in thick snow, whereas dogs can run over it. Also, ponies sweat all over their bodies, and this sweat turns to ice. Dogs sweat only through their tongues. Lastly, ponies need oats to eat, whereas dogs will happily eat dead members of the pack.

The answer here seems quite clear — as Scott found out too late, ponies are useless.

THE DEPTHS OF THE

Illustrated by CHRIS FORSEY

ON JANUARY 23, 1960, two men set out to dive to the deepest place in the world — the bottom of the Marianas Trench in the Pacific Ocean. *The History News* looks back at their astounding achievement.

REACHING THE lowest point in the world — almost 7 miles below the ocean's surface — was the goal of Swiss scientist Jacques Piccard. An experienced diver, Piccard had made many trips in his special underwater craft, called the *Trieste*, but never before had he attempted to venture so deep.

Piccard had worked for years to help his father, Auguste Piccard, develop and perfect the *Trieste*. This was to be its toughest test — the craft would be underwater for more than nine hours.

POINT OF NO RETURN

The weather was rough and stormy on the day of the descent. It had already taken four days for a United States navy tugboat to tow the *Trieste* to a point above the Marianas Trench, and

the *Trieste* had been damaged along the way.

But Piccard and his fellow crewman, a U.S. naval officer named Don Walsh, decided to go ahead with the attempt rather than face months of delay spent waiting for another opportunity.

Most of the *Trieste* consisted of a huge metal hull, called the float, which was partly filled with iron pellets that helped it to sink.

Hanging beneath the float was a small round cabin, just large enough to hold two people and the craft's controls, with large viewing windows.

At 8:23 A.M., the two men climbed into the tiny cabin and Piccard opened the hatches to allow water to flow into the float. The *Trieste* slipped

PLUMBING THE DEPTHS: The *Trieste* descends to the deepest part of the oceans.

quickly underneath the waves. Very carefully Piccard adjusted the flow of water into the hull, until the machine was descending at just over 3 feet per second.

By 2,600 feet down, the water around the *Trieste* was chilly and

completely dark. There was no sign of life.

At a depth of more than 6 miles, the silence was suddenly shattered by a loud splintering. The *Trieste* began to tremble. As Piccard reported later, he did not know what to do. Everything on board

seemed normal. "Let us go on," he finally said.

At 12:56 P.M., Piccard and Walsh first saw the ocean floor appear on their depth finder, which showed how far they were from the bottom. They had 300 feet to go.

It took them 10 long

GOING DEEPER AND DEEPER

Illustrated by MAXINE HAMIL

minutes to travel that short distance. Then at last, as Piccard stated, "At 13:06 hours the *Trieste* made a perfect landing. In the name of science and humanity, we took possession of the abyss, the last extreme on our earth that remained to be conquered."

SECRET WORLD

The two men gazed in wonder at the still world outside. The floor of the ocean was made of an ivory-colored dust, like talcum powder.

They watched as a large flat fish slowly swam away into the dark. For many years scientists had wanted to find out if fish could exist deep in the ocean. Now, in one glance, the debate was settled.

Walsh telephoned

the surface to confirm their depth. Then he discovered what had caused the bang. One of the large viewing windows had cracked, but was withstanding the water pressure.

After 20 minutes Piccard let loose a shower of iron pellets and the *Trieste* began to float upward. Gradually their speed increased.

At 2,000 feet below the surface, light began to filter through the waves. And at 4:56 P.M. the *Trieste* burst safely back into the open air, exactly on schedule.

Piccard's descent to the depths had lasted just a few hours, yet in that short time he had conquered the world's last frontier — the very bottom of the sea. ✳

LONG BEFORE THE DESCENT of the *Trieste*, people had been searching for ways to explore the ocean floor. But the ability to dive deep beneath the ocean waves demanded the invention of new machines. *The History News* charts our progress in conquering the depths.

✪ **1531:** An Italian inventor, Gugliemo de Lorena, designed the diving bell. It was lowered into the water open-end first so air was trapped inside. A diver could stay under it for up to an hour.

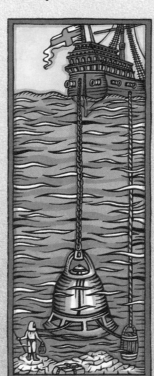

DOWN UNDER: Halley's diving bell.

✪ **1717:** A diving bell with its own supply of air was developed by the English astronomer Edmund Halley. The air was brought down in

two barrels. People could stay underwater for an hour and a half.

✪ **1865:** A Frenchman, Ernst Bazin, invented the diving shell.

The weight of water pressing on an object increases as it sinks deeper, and this weight, or pressure, can crush a diving bell.

Bazin's diving shell was made of steel and sealed all around, so it was much stronger than a diving bell. It could go down to 236 feet.

✪ **1930:** William Beebe, an American zoologist, and an engineer, Otis Barton, invented the round bubble called a bathysphere. Its shape and thick steel walls allowed it to withstand even greater pressure.

In 1934, Beebe and Barton went to a record depth of 3,027 feet.

✪ **1948:** Swiss scientist Auguste Piccard invented the bathyscaph. Bells, shells, and bathyspheres all had to be lowered

AIR BUBBLE: Beebe's bathysphere.

and lifted from the water with a heavy metal cable. This meant that nothing could go below a mile, because no winch was strong enough to lift the length of the cable needed to go deeper.

But the bathyscaph was not attached to a cable at all, so it could go far deeper than the bathysphere. It was free moving and could travel horizontally and vertically. A crew could stay underwater for up to 24 hours. The *Trieste* was an improved type of bathyscaph. ✳

WHERE TO NEXT?

TALKING about the shape of exploration today to Nigel Winser is a revelation.

Did you know that several hundred of the highest mountains, located in many parts of the world, have yet to be climbed?

Or that the huge ice caps that lie at the far north and south of the world have only just begun to be explored in any detail?

Meanwhile the vast green rooftop canopy made by the tallest trees in the rain forests is still almost totally unexplored. And today scientists have found

IT SEEMS AS IF the extremes of the earth have all been long since conquered. So what challenges are left on our planet for today's explorers? That's the question *The History News* asked Nigel Winser of the Royal Geographical Society in Great Britain.

and named less than one in ten of all the species of plants and animals in the world.

And then there are the oceans — covering more than two-thirds of the earth. We travel their surfaces, yet little is known about the ocean floor and what lives there.

Exploration today is not about finding new trade routes or settling new lands. To Nigel Winser, it is all about

trying to understand our world rather than conquer it.

WHAT MAKES OUR WORLD TICK?

He is convinced that the greatest challenge for explorers now is to discover what makes our planet work, and how all the forces of nature come together, influencing one another

and our environment.

And Nigel Winser believes it is this quest for scientific knowledge that has done the most to change the face of modern expeditions.

"It's no longer a case of setting off to seek personal glory," he says. "Now groups of people from many countries and with many different skills

work together on long-term projects. And the information that they discover is shared with anyone who wants it.

And explorers today look to many different sources for help. They use modern computers and satellites, but they also turn to the local people for traditional knowledge about the places where they live.

Exploration shall never end — we will always be questioning our world and looking for more answers." ✳

TIME LINE

☙ **1500 B.C.–A.D. 500**
The Polynesians settle islands throughout the Pacific Ocean.

☙ **750–400s B.C.**
The Phoenicians and their navy dominate the Mediterranean Sea.

☙ **470 B.C.**
Phoenician Hanno sails along the north and west coasts of Africa.

☙ **138–126 B.C.**
Chang Chi'en is the first known Chinese explorer to travel outside China.

☙ **115 B.C.**
Following Chang Chi'en's route, the Silk Road brings trade between China and the West.

☙ **A.D. 127–47**
Ptolemy lives in Egypt and researches *Geography*, his book that maps the known world.

☙ **A.D. 700s–1100s**
Viking power in northern Europe is at its height.

☙ **about 1001**
Viking Leif Eriksson sails to North America and a new settlement is started.

☙ **about 1090**
The compass is invented in China.

☙ **1325–53**
Ibn Battuta travels widely throughout the Muslim world, which stretches from Spain to India.

☙ **1487–88**
Bartholomeu Dias rounds the Cape of Good Hope at the tip of South Africa.

☙ **1492–93**
Christopher Columbus sails across the Atlantic Ocean and discovers a "New World."

☙ **1497**
John Cabot becomes the first explorer to sail to Canada.

☙ **1497–98**
Vasco da Gama sails around Africa to India.

☙ **1519–22**
Ferdinand Magellan and then Juan del Cano lead a voyage around the world.

MAGELLAN

☙ **1519–21**
Hernán Cortés invades the Aztec empire in Mexico.

☙ **1530–33**
Francisco Pizarro crushes the Incan empire in Peru.

☙ **1531**
Gugliemo de Lorena invents the diving bell.

☙ **1534–41**
Jacques Cartier explores the interior of Canada.

☙ **1538–42**
Hernando de Soto travels through Florida.

☙ **1541–42**
Francisco de Orellana sails down the Amazon River.

☙ **1607**
European settlers first arrive in North America.

☙ **1642**
Abel Tasman reaches Tasmania, New Zealand, and Fiji.

☙ **1768–71**
James Cook's first voyage to the Pacific Ocean.

☙ **1779**
Cook killed in Hawaii, during his third journey to the Pacific.

☙ **1788**
First European settlers arrive in Australia.

☙ **1804–06**
Meriwether Lewis and William Clark, helped by Sacajawea, cross North America.

☙ **1847**
John Franklin dies in the Northwest Passage.

☙ **1853–56**
David Livingstone crosses Africa from west to east.

☙ **1856–58**
John Speke reaches Lake Victoria and claims it's the source of the Nile River.

☙ **1860–61**
Robert Burke and William Wills cross Australia from south to north, but die on their return journey.

☙ **1871**
Henry Stanley meets David Livingstone at Ujiji.

☙ **1893–95**
Mary Kingsley travels in west Africa.

KINGSLEY

☙ **1903–06**
Roald Amundsen is the first person to succeed in finding a way through the Northwest Passage.

☙ **1909**
Robert Peary reaches the North Pole.

☙ **1911**
Roald Amundsen reaches the South Pole.

☙ **1912**
Robert Scott reaches the South Pole, but dies on his return journey.

☙ **1930**
William Beebe and Otis Barton invent the bathysphere.

☙ **1948**
Auguste Piccard invents the bathyscaph.

☙ **1960**
Jacques Piccard and Don Walsh reach the lowest point on the ocean floor.

Some of the dates in this book have the letters "B.C." after them. B.C. stands for "Before Christ" — so 300 B.C. means 300 years before the birth of Christ. "A.D." means after the birth of Christ.

Author: Michael Johnstone
Consultants:
Shane Winser, Royal Geographical Society, U.K.
Val Garwood, National Maritime Museum, U.K.
Editor: Lesley Ann Daniels
Designer: Louise Jackson

Advertisement illustrations by:
Vanessa Card: 4bl
Maxine Hamil: 19bm
Ian Thompson: 9br, 27tr
Micheala Stewart: 20bl
Mike White: 10bl, 25br, 27br

Decorative borders and small illustrations by:
Vanessa Card: 5, 17
Maxine Hamil: 1, 8–9, 22, 24–25, 28, 31
Micheala Stewart: 13
Mike White: 23

Photograph:
Royal Geographical Society: 30

All maps by David Atkinson

With thanks to
Linda Rogers, Linden Artists, Specs Art, Temple Rogers, The Garden Studio, Royal Geographical Society

ISBN 0-590-26675-6

Text copyright © 1997 by Michael Johnstone. Illustrations copyright © 1997 by Walker Books Ltd. All rights reserved. Published by Scholastic Inc., 555 Broadway, New York, NY 10012, by arrangement with Candlewick Press. SCHOLASTIC and associated logos are trademarks and/or registered trademarks of Scholastic Inc.

12 11 10 9 8 7 6 5 4 3
8 9/9 0 1 2 3/0

Printed in the U.S.A. 08

First Scholastic printing, January 1998

SOURCES

Roald Amundsen, *The South Pole*
Jacques Cartier, *Voyages*
Christopher Columbus, *Journal of Discovery*
James Cook, *A Voyage to the Pacific Ocean*
Hernán Cortés, *Letters from Mexico*
Ibn Battuta, *Travels*
Meriwether Lewis and William Clark, *Journals*
David Livingstone, *Expedition to the Zambezi*
Robert Peary, *The North Pole*
Jacques Piccard, *Man's Deepest Dive*
Antonia Pigafetta, *The First Voyage Round the World by Magellan*
Robert Scott, *Diaries and Letters*
Henry Stanley, *How I Found Livingstone*
William Wills, *Journal*